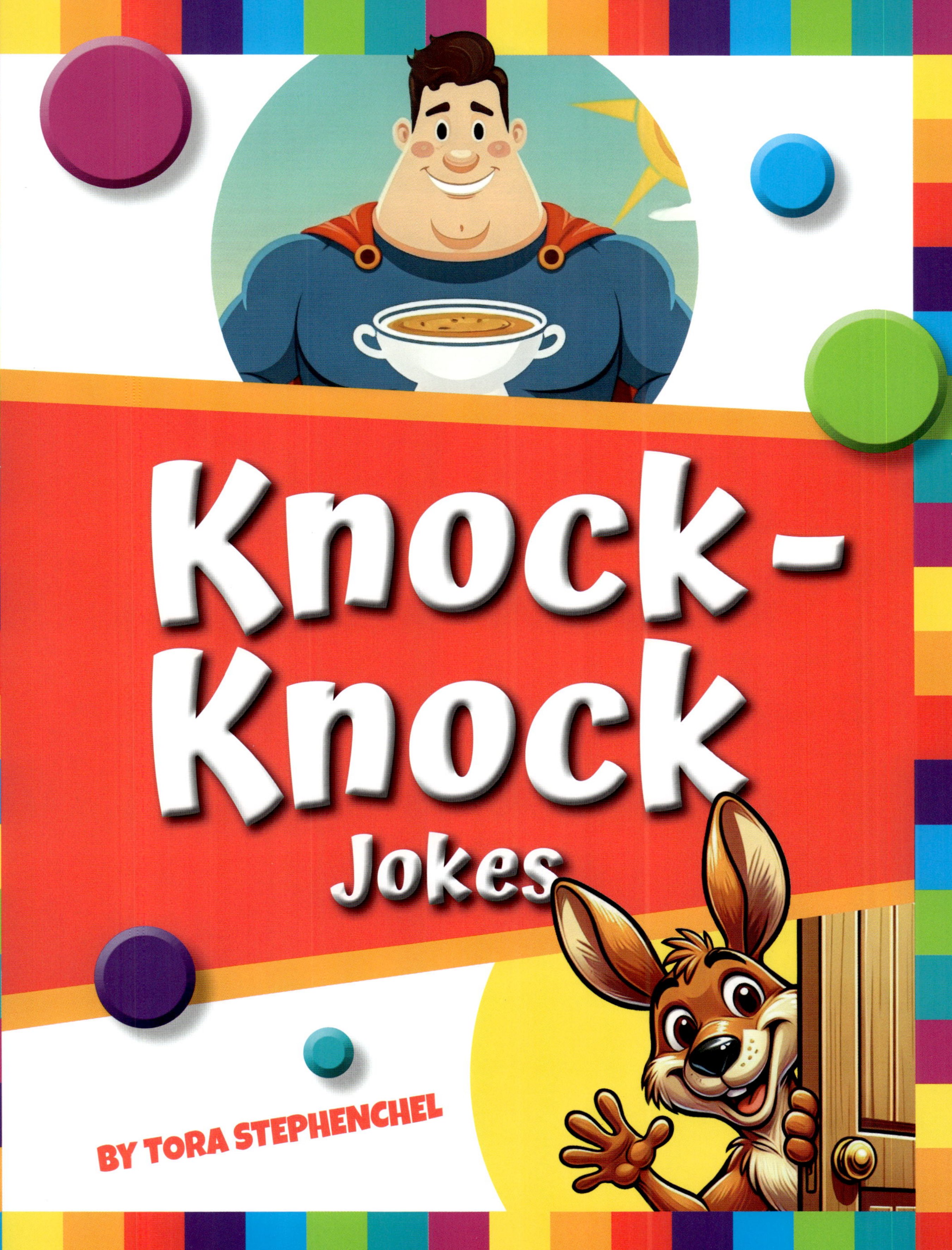
Knock-Knock
Jokes
BY TORA STEPHENCHEL

Published by The Child's World®
800-599-READ • childsworld.com

Photography Credits
All images © Shutterstock AI

ISBN Information
9781503876088 (Reinforced Library Binding)
9781503876613 (Portable Document Format)
9781503877115 (Online Multi-user eBook)
9781503877733 (Electronic Publication)

LCCN
2025938207

Printed in the United States of America

About the Author

Tora Stephenchel is a Minnesota-based author who loves to write books with just the right amount of giggles. Fueled by family adventures to everywhere from bluffs to beaches, Tora believes every book should leave young hearts a little brighter and lighter.

Knock-Knock! Who's there?

Water. Water who?

Water you doing today?

WELCOME

Knock-Knock! Who's there?

Arthur. Arthur who?

Arthur any cookies left?

Knock-Knock! Who's there?
You. You who?
Yoo-hoo! Is anybody home?

Knock-Knock! Who's there?
Soup. Soup who?
Soup-erman!

Did You Know?

Soup has been around for thousands of years. Early soups contained just **herbs** and grains. Over time, people began to add vegetables and meats.

Knock-Knock! Who's there?

Boo. Boo who?

Why are you crying?

Knock-Knock! Who's there?
Annie. Annie who?
Anniebody home?

Knock-Knock! Who's there?

Nana. Nana who?

Nana your business!

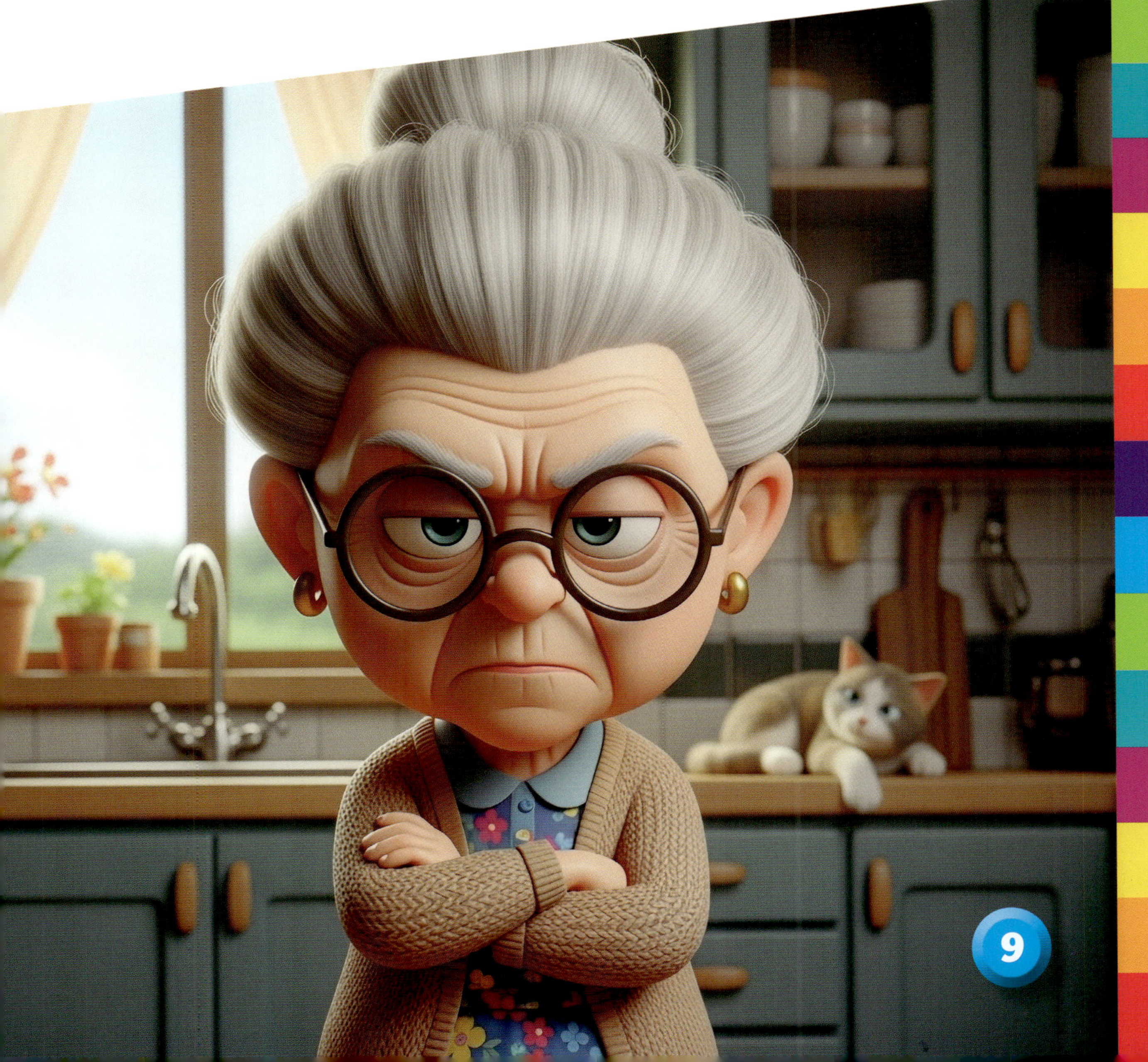

Knock-Knock! Who's there?
Waddle. Waddle who?
Waddle it take for you to open the door?

Knock-Knock! Who's there?
Kanga. Kanga who?
No, silly! It's kanga-ROO!

Knock-Knock! Who's there?
Bean. Bean who?
Bean a while since I've seen you!

Knock-Knock! Who's there?
Who. Who who?
Who! Who! You sound like an owl!

Did You Know?
Owls are **raptors**. They are also **nocturnal**. Owls make almost no noise when they fly. This helps them sneak up on their meals.

Knock-Knock! Who's there?
Weirdo. Weirdo who?
Weirdo you think you're going?

Knock-Knock! Who's there?

Ya. Ya who?

Ya-hooooo! It's time to play!

Did You Know?

Playgrounds are mostly for children. But some cities are now designing playgrounds for adults. These areas have chin-up bars and other **equipment** to help adults get exercise.

Knock-Knock! Who's there?

Cook. Cook who?

I'm not cuckoo, but I do sound silly sometimes!

Knock-Knock! Who's there?

Alex. Alex who?

Alex-plain later.
Just open the door!

Did You Know?
Orange juice is the most popular fruit juice in the world.

Knock-Knock! Who's there?
Orange. Orange who?
Orange you going to let me in?

Knock-Knock! Who's there?

Anita. Anita who?

Anita use the bathroom!

Knock-Knock! Who's there?

Giraffe. Giraffe who?

Giraffe anything to eat in there? I'm starving!

Knock-Knock! Who's there?

Howl. Howl who?

Howl you know unless you open the door?

Knock-Knock! Who's there?

Weekend. Weekend who?

Weekend do anything we want!

Knock-Knock! Who's there?
Tank. Tank who?
You're welcome.

equipment (eh-KWIP-ment) The tools or things needed to do something are called equipment.

herbs (URBZ) Herbs are plants used in cooking and medicines. Mint, dill, rosemary, and sage are all herbs.

nocturnal (nok-TUR-null) When an animal is nocturnal, it is active mostly at night and rests during the day. Owls are nocturnal.

raptors (RAP-turz) Raptors are birds that hunt and eat other animals for food. Owls are raptors.

In the Library

Elliot, Rob. *Knock-Knock Jokes for Kids.* Grand Rapids, MI: Spire, 2013.

National Geographic Kids. *Just Jokes: 591½ Rib-Tickling Riddles, Knee-Slapping Knock-Knocks, and Tricky Tongue Twisters for Kids!* Washington, DC: National Geographic Kids: 2025.

Winn, Whee. *Lots of Knock-Knock Jokes for Kids.* Grand Rapids, MI: Zonderkidz, 2016.

On the Web

Visit our website for more knock-knock jokes:
childsworld.com/links

Note to Parents, Caregivers, Teachers, and Librarians: We routinely verify our Web links to make sure they are safe and active sites. So encourage your readers to check them out!